The Boy Who Cried Wolf

Adapted by Rob M. Worley

Illustrated by Will Meugniot

WAYLAND

First published in 2014 by Wayland

Copyright © 2014 Wayland

Wayland
338 Euston Road
London NW1 3BH

Wayland Australia
Level 17/207 Kent Street
Sydney, NSW 2000

Adapted Text by Rob M. Worley
Illustrations by Will Meugniot
Colours by Carlos Badilla Z.
Edited by Stephanie Hedlund
Interior Layout by Kristen Fitzner Denton and Alyssa Peacock
Book Design and Packaging by Shannon Eric Denton
Cover Design by Alyssa Peacock

Copyright © 2008 by Abdo Consulting Group

A cataloguing record for this title is available at the British Library.
Dewey number: 398.2'452-dc23

Printed in China

ISBN: 978 0 7502 7831 7

Wayland is a division of Hachette Children's Books, an Hachette UK company.
www.hachette.co.uk

There once was a shepherd boy.

The only thing he ever saw was sheep.

The townsfolk ran to help him.

But there was no wolf.

The next day, the boy became bored again.

'He would not try to trick us twice'
the townsfolk said.

'You are so foolish to be tricked again!' the boy said.

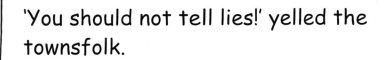

'You should not tell lies!' yelled the townsfolk.

The next day, a wolf sprang out of the woods.

20

The townsfolk thought he was trying to trick them again.

The boy wondered why nobody came to help.

Finally, the flock reached town.

'Why didn't you help me?' the boy asked.

'Because you lied to us twice before' the townsfolk said.

The moral of the story is:

Nobody believes a liar, even when he tells the truth.